Einfache Lesespurgeschichten

FÜR DEN

Englischunterricht

inkl. Zusatzmaterial

Differenzierte Geschichten

Ricarda Dransmann | Svenja Sölter

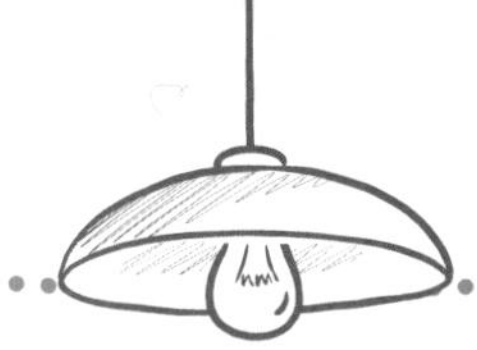

Impressum

Titel

Einfache Lesespurgeschichten für den Englischunterricht

Differenzierte Geschichten, inkl. Zusatzmaterial

Autorinnen

Ricarda Dransmann

Svenja Sölter

Umschlagmotive

Bettina Weyland

Illustrationen

soweit nicht anders angegeben. Bettina Weyland

Druck

Heenemann GmbH & Co. KG, Berlin, DE

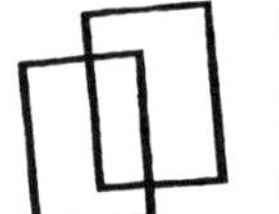

Verlag an der Ruhr
Mülheim an der Ruhr
www.verlagruhr.de

Geeignet für die Klassen 3–6

ISBN 978-3-8346-6052-7

Inhaltsverzeichnis

Vorwort

Liebe Lehrkräfte,

das Erlernen einer Fremdsprache geht am besten mit Spaß.

Deshalb ist es eine schöne Idee, den spielerischen Charakter von Lesespurgeschichten in den Englischunterricht mit einzubauen. Wir alle lernen besser und effektiver, wenn wir Freude am Lernen haben. Mithilfe von Lesespurgeschichten soll vor allem die Motivation zum Lesen gefördert und gleichzeitig der Wortschatz erweitert werden.

Lesespurgeschichten sind vergleichbar mit einer Schatzsuche: logisch denken, kombinieren und Verknüpfungen erstellen. In einem Text befinden sich versteckte Hinweise, deren Entdeckung zu einer richtigen Reihenfolge führt. Dabei gibt es auch sogenannte Sackgassen, die auf einen Fehler hinweisen, ohne dass jedoch das Spiel beendet werden muss.

Parallel zum Text arbeiten die Kinder mit einem Lesespurbild. Über dieses erhalten sie Informationen zu einer Ziffernfolge, die mithilfe eines Lösungsschlüssels ein Lösungswort ergibt. Das klingt vielleicht zu Beginn etwas kompliziert, aber haben die Kinder (und natürlich auch Sie) die Vorgehensweise erst einmal verstanden, so werden sie großen Spaß bei der Umsetzung haben.

Zielgruppe der Lesespurgeschichten sind Schüler*innen der Jahrgänge 3 bis 6 – viele Kinder können die einfachen, kurzen Texte schon in der dritten Klasse gut lesen, doch auch ältere Kinder werden hieran gleichermaßen Freude haben und ihren Wortschatz festigen können.

Lesespurgeschichten bieten eine wundervolle, spielerische und kreative Möglichkeit, Kindern Freude am Lesen zu vermitteln.

Wir wünschen Ihnen viel Spaß bei der Umsetzung!

Ricarda Dransmann & Svenja Sölter

Der Verlag an der Ruhr legt großen Wert auf eine geschlechtergerechte und inklusive Sprache. Daher nutzen wir das Gendersternchen, um sowohl männliche und weibliche als auch nichtbinäre Geschlechtsidentitäten einzuschließen. Alternativ verwenden wir neutrale Formulierungen. In Texten für Schüler*innen finden sich aus didaktischen Gründen neutrale Begriffe bzw. Doppelformen.

Einsatz der Lesespurgeschichten

Es gibt verschiedene Möglichkeiten, Lesespurgeschichten im Unterricht einzubinden. Entweder erfolgt die Umsetzung im **Klassenverband** oder in Form von **Einzel-, Zweier- oder Gruppenarbeit.**

Die Umsetzung im Klassenverband bietet sich als Einführung an. Das Bild kann z. B. mit einer digitalen Tafel für alle Kinder sichtbar gemacht werden und die Kinder erhalten die Lesetexte. Gemeinsam wird dann entweder durch die Schüler*innen oder durch die Lehrkraft der Text schrittweise vorgelesen und die richtige Lösung gesucht.

Wenn Sie sich für eine Partner- oder Gruppenarbeit entscheiden, dann empfiehlt es sich, leistungsstärkere mit leistungsschwächeren Kindern zu kombinieren. Die leistungsstärkeren Kinder können dann die Vorleserolle übernehmen und die leistungsschwächeren Kinder hören genau zu und versuchen, den Hinweisen zu folgen.

Bevor Sie die Kinder selbstständig mit den Lesespurgeschichten arbeiten lassen, ist es von besonderer Bedeutung, dass alle die Vorgehensweise verstanden haben. Besonders bewährt hat sich während der Einführung die Methode/Rollenfunktion einer **Lesespurexpertin** oder eines **Lesespurexperten**. Dieses Kind kann die Mitschüler*innen bei Verständnisschwierigkeiten unterstützen und entlastet Sie als Lehrkraft. Hier empfiehlt es sich, ein Kind auszuwählen, dass z. B. Lesespurgeschichten schon aus anderen Unterrichtsfächern kennt oder aber bereits die eingesetzte Lesespurgeschichte bearbeitet hat. Es könnte aber auch bei einfachen Fragen zum Verständnis seinen Mitschüler*innen mit der Wörterliste helfen.

Im Anschluss an die Erklärungseinheit können Sie den Einsatz von Lesespurgeschichten in Ihren Unterricht frei einplanen. Es ist dabei ganz Ihnen überlassen, ob Sie die Materialien im Unterricht/ Wochenplan oder bei ähnlichen Methoden nutzen.

Für die Bearbeitung einer Lesespurgeschichte benötigt jedes Kind folgende Materialien:

- **Anleitung** „So geht's!" (S. 7)
  Zum besseren Verständnis ist diese Anleitung ausnahmsweise auf Deutsch verfasst.
- **Lesespurgeschichte**
  In diesem Buch finden Sie insgesamt sechs verschiedene Lesespurgeschichten. Jede Geschichte liegt in 2-facher Differenzierung vor (siehe „Differenzierung", S. 6).
- **Lesespurkarte** (S. 56)
  Die Lesespurkarte kann genutzt werden, um zu jedem Abschnitt die Schlüsselwörter einzutragen, die zum nächsten Abschnitt führen sollen. Es hilft den Kindern, den Überblick zu behalten und mögliche Fehler schneller zurückzuverfolgen.
- **Lesespurbild** (hinten im Buch ab S. 69)
  Zu jeder Lesespurgeschichte gehört ein passendes Lesespurbild. Die Lesespurbilder zu allen Geschichten finden Sie hinten im Buch sowohl in Farbe als auch in schwarz-weiß. Sie können frei entscheiden, ob Sie das farbige Bild nehmen oder lieber (z. B. weil kein Farbdrucker vorliegt) auf die Schwarz-Weiß-Variante zurückgreifen. Wir empfehlen, jedem Kind eine Kopie des Lesespurbilds auszuhändigen. Alternativ können Sie es aber auch mehrfach im Klassenraum aufhängen oder projizieren.
- **Lösungsschlüssel** (hinter den jeweiligen Lesespurgeschichten zu finden)
  Mithilfe des Lösungsschlüssels können die Kinder ihre *reading steps* bzw. die Zahlenfolge in ein Lösungswort umwandeln. Dies dient der Selbstkontrolle. Eine Übersicht über alle richtigen Lösungswörter und die richtigen *reading steps* finden Sie auf S. 57–59.
- **Wörterliste** (hinter den jeweiligen Lesespurgeschichten zu finden)
  Die Wörterliste ist in alphabetischer Reihenfolge abgebildet und dient zum Verständnis noch unbekannter Wörter.

Einsatz der Lesespurgeschichten

✓ **Übungen** (hinter den jeweiligen Lesespurgeschichten zu finden)
Im Anschluss an die Bearbeitung der Lesespurgeschichte bieten sich weiterführende Übungen an. Sie finden hier immer ein Blatt mit Übungen zum Textverständnis *(reading comprehension)* und eines mit zusätzlichen Aufgaben zur Vertiefung der Wortfelder *(worksheet)*. **Lösungen** zu den Übungen finden Sie ab S. 60.

Differenzierung

Jede der sechs Lesespurgeschichten ist in **zwei differenzierten Versionen** vorhanden. Gekennzeichnet wurden diese mit den neutralen Symbolen Schleife (für die leichtere Differenzierungsstufe) und Geschenk (für die etwas detailliertere Differenzierungsstufe).

Wie unterscheiden sich die differenzierten Lesespurgeschichten voneinander?

Diese Differenzierungsstufe enthält weniger Text sowie einen sehr einfachen und kurzen Satzbau. Die Schlüsselbegriffe sind bereits fett gedruckt, sodass sie für die Kinder leicht identifizierbar sind. Auf abgekürzte Verbformen wurde verzichtet, Zahlen werden als Nummer geschrieben.

Diese Differenzierungsstufe ist detaillierter verfasst und enthält etwas komplexere Satzstrukturen. Die Schlüsselbegriffe werden nicht hervorgehoben. Außerdem werden abgekürzte Verbformen benutzt und Zahlen als Zahlwort verwendet.

Umsetzung der Lesespurgeschichte

Eine Lesespurgeschichte besteht aus mehreren Teilen, die durch Lesen und Abgleichen mit dem Lesespurbild in eine richtige Reihenfolge gebracht werden müssen. Ziel ist das Trainieren der genauen Lesefähigkeiten sowie der Festigung des englischen Wortschatzes unter spielerischen Bedingungen.

So geht man vor:

1. Die Kinder legen die **Lesespurgeschichte** (in der jeweiligen Differenzierungsstufe) sowie das **Lesespurbild** (schwarz-weiß oder farbig) vor sich hin, sodass sie beide Blätter parallel betrachten können. Zudem nehmen sie einen Stift in die Hand. Es empfiehlt sich, hierfür einen Bleistift zu nehmen, damit eventuelle Korrekturen einfach durchgeführt werden können.
2. Die Kinder lesen die kurze Einführung und den ersten Abschnitt. In diesem Abschnitt befindet sich der erste **Schlüsselbegriff**.
3. Mit dem Schlüsselbegriff im Kopf wenden sich die Kinder mit ihren Blicken dem Lesespurbild zu und suchen die dazu **passende Abbildung.** Beispiel: Der versteckte Schlüsselbegriff lautet „dog" – so wird auf dem Lesespurbild der Hund gesucht.
4. Hat das Kind die richtige Abbildung gefunden, so notiert es die an der Abbildung befindliche **Lesespurziffer** unter **Reading steps** unten unter der Lesespurgeschichte. Alternativ kann dafür auch die ebenfalls in diesem Werk enthaltene **Lesespurkarte** (S. 56) im Sinne einer Gedächtnisstütze verwendet werden. Hiermit können eventuelle Korrekturen später etwas einfacher durchgeführt werden.
5. Die Kinder nutzen nun die Ziffer als Hinweis für den **nächsten zu lesenden Abschnitt.** Beispiel: Neben dem Hund auf dem Lesespurbild steht die Ziffer 4. Die Kinder lesen dann bei Abschnitt 4 weiter. So geht es immer weiter, bis eine 10-stellige Lesespur verfolgt wurde. Achtung, punktuell befinden sich **Irrwege** in den Lesespurgeschichten. Diesen gilt es auszuweichen, denn nicht alle Textabschnitte sind Teil der Geschichte.
6. Die Zahlenfolge kann am Ende mithilfe des **Lösungsschlüssels,** der sich immer hinter den Lesespurgeschichten in diesem Buch befindet, in Buchstaben umgewandelt werden. Daraus ergibt sich ein **Lösungswort,** welches den Schüler*innen gleichzeitig die Möglichkeit der Selbstkontrolle gewährt.

Anleitung: So geht's ...!

Reading tracks are fun – they are easily done!

- Starte mit dem Lesen der **Überschrift und der kleinen Einführung.** Sie geben dir einen ersten Einblick in das Thema der Lesespurgeschichte.
- Lies nun den **ersten Abschnitt** und suche nach **einem Schlüsselbegriff.**
- Mit dem Schlüsselbegriff im Kopf suchst du nun mit deinen Augen die **passende Abbildung** auf deinem Lesespurbild.
  Beispiel: Der versteckte Schlüsselbegriff lautet „dog". Du suchst also auf dem Lesespurbild nach einem Hund.
- Neben der Abbildung befindet sich eine Zahl. Diese sagt dir, an welcher Stelle es weitergeht und welchen Abschnitt du nun lesen sollst.
  Beispiel: Neben dem Hund steht eine 4. Du liest also bei Textabschnitt 4 weiter.
- Notiere die Zahl des Abschnitts auf der Lesespurgeschichte unter **reading steps** oder nutze dafür die Lesespurkarte.
- Suche nun das nächste Schlüsselwort und die passende Abbildung, bis du am **Ende der Lesespur** ankommst.
- Wandle die Zahlenfolge mithilfe des **Lösungsschlüssels** in Buchstaben um. Daraus ergibt sich ein Lösungswort."

Tipps

Manchmal kann es sein, dass du dich auf einem Irrweg befindest. Nicht schlimm!
Lies noch einmal genau. Nutze auch deine Wörterliste als Hilfestellung.

Name

Datum

In the pet shop (1/2)

Story

Maja wants a new pet. Maja and her mother go to the pet shop.

Start at number 1.

1 Maja's mother says, "Look, Maja! What a nice **cat**!"

2 Sorry, that is a **tortoise**. You are wrong here. Read again.

3 The fish tank is too expensive. Maja goes to the **guinea pig**.

4 The shop assistant says, "Hello!"
Maja says, "I want a new pet. Maybe a **dog**?"

5 Oh no, this is a **rabbit**. Maja does not look for a rabbit.
Read again.

6 This is not the shop assistant; it is **grandfather** Bill.
Read number 15 again.

7 The fishes are cool. "But then I need a **fish tank**," says Maja.

8 This is the guinea pig. But it is already sold. Maja sees
a **budgie**.

9 This is a **parrot**. You are wrong here. Read again.

In the pet shop (2/2)

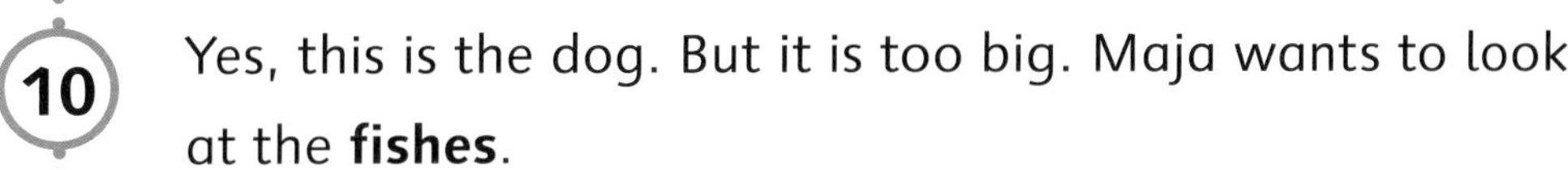

10 Yes, this is the dog. But it is too big. Maja wants to look at the **fishes**.

11 The bird cage is nice. Maja pays with her birthday **money**.

12 This is not a cage for a budgie.
This is a **cage** for a **hamster**. Read number 13 again.

13 The budgie is perfect for Maja. "I need a **bird cage**, too," says Maja.

14 **Maja** is very happy. She has got a new pet!

15 Yes, this is the cat. But Maja does not like cats.
Maja and her mother go to the **shop assistant**.

Reading steps: (1) ( ) ( ) ( ) ( ) ( ) ( ) ( ) ( ) ( )

Solution words: A budgie eats ....

and ....

Name

Datum

In the pet shop (1/2)

Story

It was Maja's birthday and she saved some money.
Now she wants to buy a pet. Maja and her mother go to the pet shop.

Start at number 1.

1 Maja and her mother are in a pet shop.
Maja's mother says, "Look, Maja! There is a nice cat!"

2 Sorry, but that's a tortoise. You're on the wrong track.
Read again.

3 The fish tank is too expensive. "Oh, mum, look!
The fluffy guinea pig! It's so cute!" says Maja.

4 The shop assistant is very nice. He says, "Hello, can I help you?"
Maja says, "I want to buy a new pet. But I don't like the cat.
Do you have a dog?"

5 No, this is a rabbit. Maja doesn't look for a rabbit.
Read again carefully.

6 Oh, that's grandfather Bill. He can't help to find a new pet.
Read number fifteen again.

7 The fishes are very colourful.
"But I need a fish tank for the fishes," says Maja.

8 "Sorry, the guinea pig is already sold," says the shop assistant.
"What about a budgie?"

In the pet shop (2/2)

9 This is a nice parrot, but you're wrong here. Read again.

10 The dog is cute. But Maja's mother says, "The dog is too big for our flat. Let's look at the fishes."

11 The bird cage is perfect for Maja's new budgie. She pays with her birthday money.

12 This isn't a cage for a budgie, it's for a hamster. Read number thirteen again.

13 The budgie is perfect for Maja. "I love the budgie! I need a bird cage for it, too," says Maja.

14 Maja is very happy because she has got a new pet – a budgie!

15 This is the cat. Maja's mother likes the cat, but Maja doesn't. They go to the shop assistant and ask for help.

Reading steps: (1) ( ) ( ) ( ) ( ) ( ) ( ) ( ) ( ) ( )

Solution words: A budgie eats ....

and ....

In the pet shop

Answer key

1	stands for	G
2	stands for	D
3	stands for	S
4	stands for	A
5	stands for	E
6	stands for	H
7	stands for	N
8	stands for	C
9	stands for	F
10	stands for	I
11	stands for	R
12	stands for	L
13	stands for	O
14	stands for	N
15	stands for	R

In the pet shop

List of words

English	German
again	noch einmal
already sold	bereits verkauft
answer key	Lösungsschlüssel
(to) ask for help	um Hilfe bitten
budgie	Wellensittich
(to) buy	kaufen
cage	Käfig
carefully	sorgfältig, aufmerksam
colourful	bunt
corn	Mais
cute	niedlich
expensive	teuer
fish tank	Aquarium
flat	Wohnung
fluffy	weich, flauschig
grains	Körner
guinea pig	Meerschweinchen
maybe	vielleicht
money	Geld
on the wrong track	auf dem falschen Weg
parrot	Papagei
(to) pay	bezahlen
(to) save	sparen
shop assistant	Verkäufer, Verkäuferin
tortoise	Schildkröte

In the pet shop

Reading comprehension

Tick the right box.

1. Maja wants
- [ ] a new T-shirt.
- [ ] a new pet.
- [ ] a new bag.

2. Maja's mother likes
- [ ] the guinea pig.
- [ ] the dog.
- [ ] the cat.

3. The dog is
- [ ] too big.
- [ ] too small.
- [ ] too expensive.

4. The fish tank is
- [ ] too cheap.
- [ ] too expensive.
- [ ] too old.

5. Maja can't buy the guinea pig because
- [ ] her mother does not like it.
- [ ] it is too big.
- [ ] it is already sold.

6. Maja's new pet needs
- [ ] a bird cage.
- [ ] a hamster cage.
- [ ] a fish tank.

7. Maja pays with her
- [ ] pocket money.
- [ ] birthday money.
- [ ] sweets.

8. Maja's new pet is
- [ ] a dog.
- [ ] a budgie.
- [ ] a hamster.

In the pet shop

Worksheet

1. Write the correct numbers.

1 parrot	2 cat	3 dog
4 fish	5 mouse	6 rabbit
7 guinea pig	8 budgie	9 tortoise

Ted

2. Find the pet words. Circle.

mousefishguineapigcatbudgierabbitdogtortoiseparrothamster

3. Read and draw.

two brown cats

four yellow fishes

a colourful parrot

4. What's your favourite pet? Write and draw.

My favourite pet is ....

Name

Datum

A crazy school day (1/2)

Story

Mrs. Miller sits at her desk. She watches the class.
Something is different today ...

Start at number 1.

1 All pupils do something different.
One **girl** reads a **comic**.

2 This is a **school bag**. You are wrong here. Read again.

3 This **pencil case** is **not black**. Read number 4 again.

4 Susan's coloured pencils are on the floor.
Mrs. Miller says, "Where is your **black pencil case**?"

5 This is a **paintbox**. We do not need it now. Read again.

6 Oh no, this **girl** reads a **book**, not a comic.
Read number 1 again.

7 Very good, this is a glue stick.
But look! Jim cuts his bread with his **scissors**!

8 Yes, this is Susan's black pencil case. But look! A **boy** wants to stick something on a piece of paper with a **ruler**.

9 This is the boy with the ruler.
Mrs. Miller says, "You need a **glue stick**."

A crazy school day (2/2)

10 Yes, Susan reads a comic.
She wants to paint it with her **coloured pencils**.

11 This is **chalk**. You are wrong here. Read again.

12 "Why is there a bin on the table?" asks Mrs. Miller.
She looks at the **blackboard**.

13 "Jim! Do not cut your bread with your scissors!" says Mrs. Miller.
She looks around. **Mira** sits **under her table**.

14 The **blackboard** says it is Sunday.
Puh! It was a crazy dream!

15 This is Mira under her table.
But what is on the table: a **bin**?

Reading steps: (1) ( ) ( ) ( ) ( ) ( ) ( ) ( ) ( ) ( )

Solution word: You need a ....

.... for your watercolours.

Name

Datum

A crazy school day (1/2)

Story

Mrs. Miller sits at her desk in the classroom and watches the class.
Today is a crazy day. Something is different ...

Start at number 1.

1. All pupils in Mrs. Miller's class do something different. One girl reads a comic.

2. We don't look for a school bag. Read again carefully.

3. This is a pencil case, but it isn't black. Read number four again.

4. Susan's coloured pencils are on the floor. Oh no! Mrs. Miller says, "Put your coloured pencils back into your black pencil case."

5. This is a paintbox with watercolours. But we don't need that now. Read again carefully.

6. This girl reads a book, but we look for a girl with a comic. Read number one again.

7. Very good, this is a glue stick. But now there is a new problem: Jim cuts his bread with his scissors!

8. Yes, this is Susan's black pencil case. But Mrs. Miller is confused: What is that? A boy takes a ruler to stick something on a piece of paper.

9. This is the boy with the ruler. Mrs. Miller says, "Don't take your ruler to stick something. You need a glue stick."

A crazy school day (2/2)

10 Yes, Susan sits in the classroom and reads a comic. She wants to paint it with her new coloured pencils.

11 This is chalk for the blackboard. Sorry, you're wrong here. Read again carefully.

12 "Why is there a bin on the table?" asks Mrs. Miller. What a crazy day! She turns around and looks at the blackboard.

13 "Jim! Don't cut your bread with your scissors!" says Mrs. Miller. She looks around in the classroom again and sees Mira. But she sits under her table!

14 The blackboard says it's Sunday today. Puh! It was just a crazy dream! Mrs. Miller is relieved.

15 This is Mira and she sits under her table. And look what's on the table: There is a bin!

Reading steps: (1) ( ) ( ) ( ) ( ) ( ) ( ) ( ) ( ) ( )

Solution word: You need a ....

.... for your watercolours.

A crazy school day

Answer key

1	stands for	P
2	stands for	M
3	stands for	E
4	stands for	I
5	stands for	O
6	stands for	L
7	stands for	B
8	stands for	N
9	stands for	T
10	stands for	A
11	stands for	G
12	stands for	S
13	stands for	R
14	stands for	H
15	stands for	U

A crazy school day

List of words

English	German
again	noch einmal
answer key	Lösungsschlüssel
bin	Mülleimer
blackboard	Tafel
carefully	sorgfältig, aufmerksam
chalk	Kreide
coloured pencils	Buntstifte
confused	verwirrt
crazy	verrückt
(to) cut	schneiden
different	anders
dream	Traum
floor	Fußboden
glue stick	Klebestift
(to) look around	sich umsehen
(to) paint	malen, anmalen
paintbox	Malkasten
paint brush	Malpinsel
(to) put … back	… zurücklegen
(a) piece of paper	(ein) Blatt Papier
relieved	erleichtert
scissors	Schere
(to) stick something	etwas aufkleben
(to) turn around	sich umdrehen
watercolours	Wasserfarben

A crazy school day

Reading comprehension

Tick the right box.

1. The teacher is called
- ☐ Mrs. Schiller.
- ☐ Mrs. Miller.
- ☐ Mrs. Thriller.

2. Susan reads
- ☐ a comic.
- ☐ a book.
- ☐ a newspaper.

3. The coloured pencils are
- ☐ on the table.
- ☐ in Susan's school bag.
- ☐ on the floor.

4. Susan's pencil case is
- ☐ blue.
- ☐ white.
- ☐ black.

5. A boy takes a ruler to stick something on
- ☐ a piece of paper.
- ☐ a table.
- ☐ a folder.

6. Jim cuts his bread
- ☐ with his knife.
- ☐ with his ruler.
- ☐ with his scissors.

7. The bin is
- ☐ on the table.
- ☐ under the table.
- ☐ behind the table.

8. The blackboard says
- ☐ it is Monday.
- ☐ it is Sunday.
- ☐ it is Saturday.

A crazy school day

Worksheet

1. Fill in the right words.

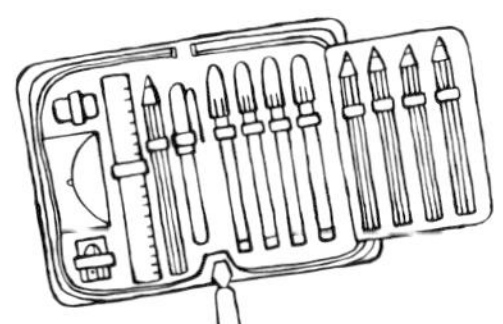

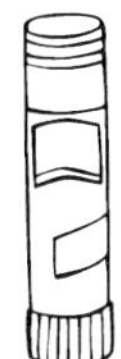

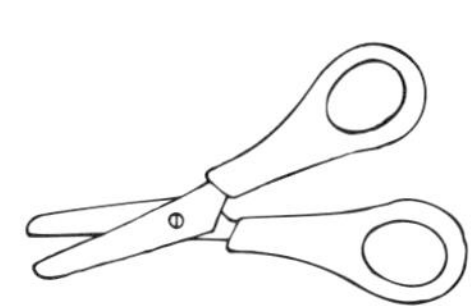

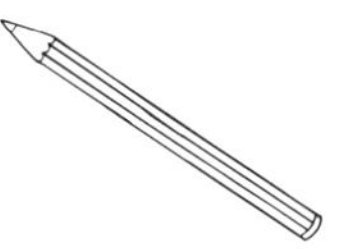

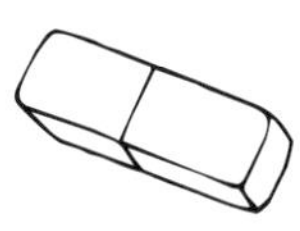

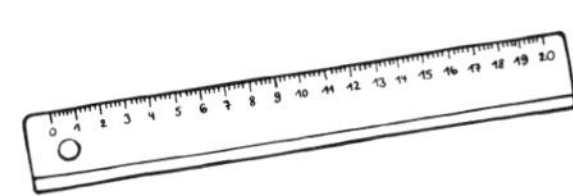

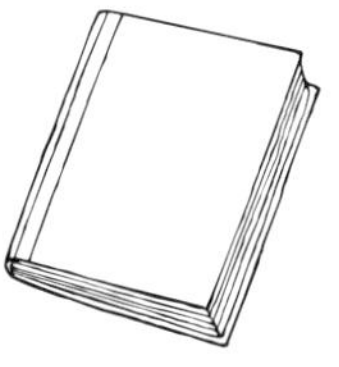

ruler | book | pencil case | glue | scissors | blackboard | rubber | pencil

2. Find the school words. Circle.

rubberschoolbaggluerulerbookpencilblackboardscissors

3. Do you know the school words? Write.

okbo .... luerr ....

clinpe .... ssssicro ....

ckalbbardo .... buberr ....

4. Write about your school bag.

In my school bag there are ....

....

Name

Datum

In the shopping mall (1/2)

Story

Linda and her father are in the shopping mall.
They go to the clothing shop.

Start at number 1.

1 Linda says, "Oh dad, look! There is a nice **dress**!"

2 "The tights are great! Let us look for a new **T-shirt**, too," Linda says.

3 Linda does not want a **pullover**. Read again.

4 This is not the shop assistant; it is a **police officer**. Read number 12 again.

5 "Yes, you can have new shoes," says Linda's father. "And here are new **white socks**."

6 There are so many T-shirts! Linda takes a T-shirt with dots. She says, "And I need a new **skirt**."

7 Linda and her father do not want a **scarf**. Read again.

8 Linda tries on a dress with flowers. Her father sees **tights**.

9 These are **black socks**. You are wrong here. Read number 5 again.

In the shopping mall (2/2)

10 No, we do not look for a **jacket**. Read again.

11 The skirt is okay, but it is too small. Linda's father shows her a **cap**.

12 Linda's father says, "No, I do not want new jeans. I am tired.
Let us pay at the **shop assistant**."

13 "Wow, dad, I look very cool with the cap!
Can I have new **shoes**, too?" Linda asks.

14 "I do not like the white socks," Linda says.
"Do you need new **jeans**, dad?"

15 Linda and her father pay at the **shop assistant** and go home.

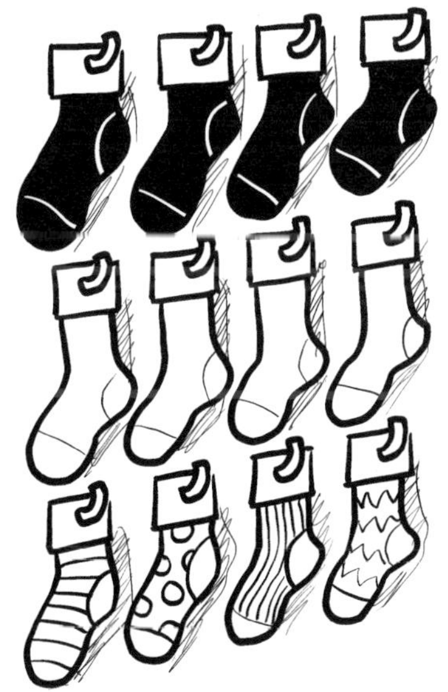

Reading steps: (1) ( ) ( ) ( ) ( ) ( ) ( ) ( ) ( ) ( )

Solution word: Linda's father still needs a

....

Name

Datum

In the shopping mall (1/2)

Story

It's Saturday. Linda and her father are in the shopping mall.
Linda needs some new clothes. They go to the clothing shop.

Start at number 1.

1. Linda and her father look around. Linda says, "Oh dad, look at the beautiful dresses! This one is a really nice dress!"

2. "The tights are perfect. I love the colour! Let's go on and look for a new T-shirt, too," Linda says.

3. The pullover is cool, but you're wrong here. Read again carefully.

4. This is a nice person, but it's not the shop assistant – it's a police officer. Read number twelve again.

5. "Of course, you can have a pair of new shoes. They look really nice," says Linda's father. "And here are new white socks."

6. There are so many colourful T-shirts with nice patterns. Linda takes a T-shirt with dots. She says, "I need a new skirt, too."

7. Linda and her father don't look for a scarf now. Read again carefully.

8. Linda tries on a dress with flowers. Her father sees matching tights and takes them to Linda.

9. These are black socks. They look good, but you are wrong here. Read number five again.

In the shopping mall (2/2)

10 Linda and her father don't need a jacket. Read again carefully.

11 Linda finds a short skirt, but it's too small. Her father shows her a cap with a zigzag pattern.

12 "No, I don't want new jeans. Shopping makes me tired. Let's pay at the shop assistant and go home," Linda's father says.

13 "Wow, dad, I look very cool with the cap. I like the zigzag pattern. Can I have new shoes, too?" Linda asks.

14 "Sorry, but I don't like the white socks," Linda says. "But dad, you need new clothes, too! Maybe a jeans?"

15 Linda and her father pay at the shop assistant and go home. What a nice shopping day!

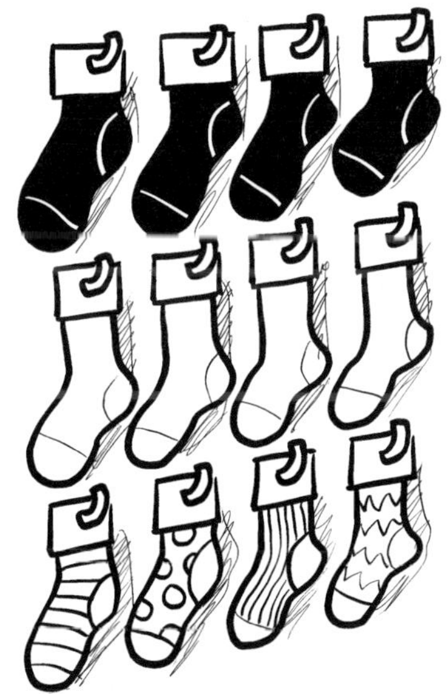

Reading steps: 1 ◯ ◯ ◯ ◯ ◯ ◯ ◯ ◯ ◯

Solution word: Linda's father still needs a

....

In the shopping mall

Answer key

1	stands for	S
2	stands for	E
3	stands for	P
4	stands for	F
5	stands for	H
6	stands for	A
7	stands for	V
8	stands for	W
9	stands for	K
10	stands for	L
11	stands for	T
12	stands for	R
13	stands for	S
14	stands for	I
15	stands for	T

In the shopping mall

List of words

English	German
again	noch einmal
answer key	Lösungsschlüssel
beautiful	schön
carefully	sorgfältig, aufmerksam
clothing shop	Kleidungsgeschäft
colourful	bunt
dots	Punkte
flowers	Blumen
(to) look around	sich umsehen/umschauen
matching	passend
of course	natürlich
(a) pair (of new shoes)	(ein) Paar (neue Schuhe)
pattern	Muster
(to) pay	bezahlen
police officer	Polizist, Polizistin
really	wirklich
scarf	Schal
short	kurz
shop assistant	Verkäufer, Verkäuferin
shopping mall	Einkaufszentrum
(to) show	zeigen
skirt	Rock
small	klein
socks	Socken
still	immer noch
tights	Strumpfhose
tired	müde
(to) try on	probieren
zigzag	Zickzack

In the shopping mall

Reading comprehension

Tick the right box.

1. Linda is in the shopping mall with
- ☐ her mother.
- ☐ her father.
- ☐ her sister.

2. Linda tries on a dress with
- ☐ flowers.
- ☐ rainbows.
- ☐ birds.

3. Linda takes a T-shirt
- ☐ with stripes.
- ☐ with dots.
- ☐ with checks.

4. The skirt is
- ☐ too big.
- ☐ too long.
- ☐ too small.

5. Linda's father sees new
- ☐ black socks.
- ☐ blue socks.
- ☐ white socks.

6. Linda's father does not want
- ☐ new socks.
- ☐ new jeans.
- ☐ new shoes.

7. At the end, Linda's father is
- ☐ angry.
- ☐ sad.
- ☐ tired.

8. Linda and her father pay at the shop assistant and
- ☐ go home.
- ☐ go to the next shop.
- ☐ go to a restaurant.

In the shopping mall

Worksheet

1. Draw lines.

- cap
- tights
- skirt
- pullover
- socks
- dress
- T-shirt
- jeans
- jacket

2. Find the words for clothes. Circle.

dresstightssocksskirtscarfjeanscapshoespulloverjacket

3. Find the odd one out. Circle.

a) jacket – pullover – socks – T-shirt

b) T-shirt – trousers – jeans – tights

c) trousers – skirt – shorts – jeans

d) socks – shorts – trousers – cap

4. Fill in the right words.

pullover (2x)
shoes
stripes
shopping mall
shop assistant

Jonas and his mother are in the ....

Jonas says, "For winter, I need a warm ...."

Jonas takes a .... with ....

His mother says, "And look at your old sneakers!

You need new ...., too." At the end, Jonas

and his mother pay at the .... and go home.

Name	Datum	

At the market (1/2)

Story

Mr. Baker goes to the market with his children. They want to buy fruits for a smoothie and vegetables for a potato soup.

Start at number 1.

1 Mr. Baker and his children, Jenny and Ron, go to the market stall.
"Hello. We need 4 **apples**, please."

2 The family does not need a **melon**. Read again.

3 "Here you are. Some grapes," says the market seller.
"And we need 8 **potatoes** for our soup."

4 "An onion for you. Do you need **peas**, too?" asks the market seller.

5 "Here you are, the apples," says the market seller.
"And 2 **bananas**, please," says Jenny.

6 The market seller gives Mr. Baker the potatoes.
"And 3 **carrots**, please," says Mr. Baker.

7 Oh, **lettuce** is wrong for a soup. Read again.

8 The market seller gives Jenny 2 bananas.
The family needs some **grapes**, too.

At the market (2/2)

9 "No, I do not like tomatoes," says Jenny.
Mr. Baker takes his **basket**.

10 "The carrots look fantastic. And an **onion**, please," says Mr. Baker.

11 "Yes, peas are great."
"Would you like some **tomatoes**, too?" says the market seller.

12 The family does not need **pears**. Read again.

13 These are **mushrooms**. Sorry, you are wrong here. Read again.

14 This is **cauliflower**. You are wrong here. Read again.

15 This is the **basket** with the fruits and vegetables.
"That is all," says Mr. Baker. "Thank you! Goodbye."

Reading steps: 1 ○ ○ ○ ○ ○ ○ ○ ○ ○

Solution word: Mr. Baker's favourite fruits are

....

Name

Datum

At the market (1/2)

Story

It's Tuesday and Mr. Baker goes to the market with his children. They want to buy fruits for a healthy smoothie and some vegetables for a potato soup.

Start at number 1.

1 Mr. Baker and his children, Jenny and Ron, go to the fruit and vegetable stall. "Hello! We need four apples for our smoothie, please."

2 This is a melon, but the family doesn't need one. Read again carefully.

3 "Here you are. Some juicy grapes," says the market seller. "Thank you. We need eight potatoes for our soup."

4 "Here you are, an onion. Do you need peas for your soup, too?" asks the market seller.

5 "Four apples. Here you are," says the market seller. "Thank you," says Mr. Baker. "And we want two bananas for the smoothie, please," says Jenny.

6 The market seller gives Mr. Baker and his children the potatoes. "Anything else?" he asks. "Oh yes, we need three carrots, please," says Mr. Baker.

7 The family wants to make a soup and doesn't need lettuce. Read again carefully.

8 The market seller gives Jenny two bananas. "Thank you!" she says. The family needs some grapes, too.

At the market (2/2)

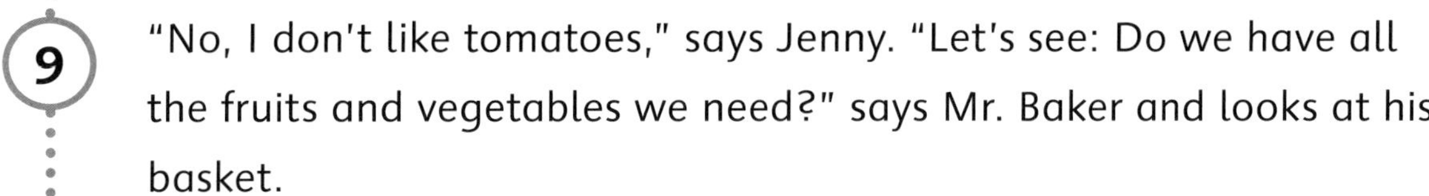

9 "No, I don't like tomatoes," says Jenny. "Let's see: Do we have all the fruits and vegetables we need?" says Mr. Baker and looks at his basket.

10 "Oh, the carrots look fantastic. And we would like to buy an onion, please," says Mr. Baker.

11 "Yes, peas are great for our soup." "Here you are. Would you like to buy some tomatoes, too?" asks the market seller.

12 These are pears. Sorry, but you are wrong here. Read again.

13 These are mushrooms. They look good, but the family doesn't want to buy them. Read again carefully.

14 This is cauliflower. You are on the wrong track. Read again carefully.

15 This is the basket full of all the fruits and vegetables. "Great, that's all," says Mr. Baker. "Thank you! Goodbye."

Reading steps: (1) ( ) ( ) ( ) ( ) ( ) ( ) ( ) ( ) ( )

Solution word: Mr. Baker's favourite fruits are

....

At the market

Answer key

1	stands for	P
2	stands for	M
3	stands for	E
4	stands for	P
5	stands for	I
6	stands for	A
7	stands for	O
8	stands for	N
9	stands for	E
10	stands for	P
11	stands for	L
12	stands for	B
13	stands for	R
14	stands for	K
15	stands for	S

At the market

List of words

English	German
again	noch einmal
answer key	Lösungsschlüssel
anything else	(sonst) noch etwas
basket	Korb
(to) buy	kaufen
carefully	sorgfältig, aufmerksam
cauliflower	Blumenkohl
full of …	voll/gefüllt mit …
(to) give	geben
grapes	Trauben
healthy	gesund
Here you are.	Bitte schön.
juicy	saftig
lettuce	Salat
market	Markt/Marktplatz
market seller	Marktverkäufer, Marktverkäuferin
mushrooms	Pilze
on the wrong track	auf dem falschen Weg
onion	Zwiebel
pears	Birnen
peas	Erbsen
(potato) soup	(Kartoffel-)Suppe
stall	Stand
That's all.	Das ist alles.
We would like …	Wir hätten gern …
Would you like…?	Hätten Sie gern/Hättest du gern …?

At the market

Reading comprehension

⊗ Tick the right box.

1. The Bakers go to
- ☐ the market.
- ☐ the shopping mall.
- ☐ the supermarket.

2. The family wants to make
- ☐ a mushroom soup.
- ☐ a potato soup.
- ☐ a tomato soup.

3. The Bakers buy fruits for
- ☐ a fruit salad.
- ☐ a cake.
- ☐ a smoothie.

4. The Bakers are
- ☐ Mr. Baker, Jimmy and Tom.
- ☐ Mrs. Baker, Jenny and Ron.
- ☐ Mr. Baker, Jenny and Ron.

5. Mr. Baker wants to buy
- ☐ 2 potatoes.
- ☐ 8 potatoes.
- ☐ 7 potatoes.

6. The carrots look
- ☐ terrible.
- ☐ good.
- ☐ fantastic.

7. Jenny does not like
- ☐ bananas.
- ☐ tomatoes.
- ☐ onions.

8. The fruits and vegetables are in
- ☐ the basket.
- ☐ the bag.
- ☐ the buggy.

At the market

Worksheet

1. What is a fruit, what is a vegetable? Draw lines.

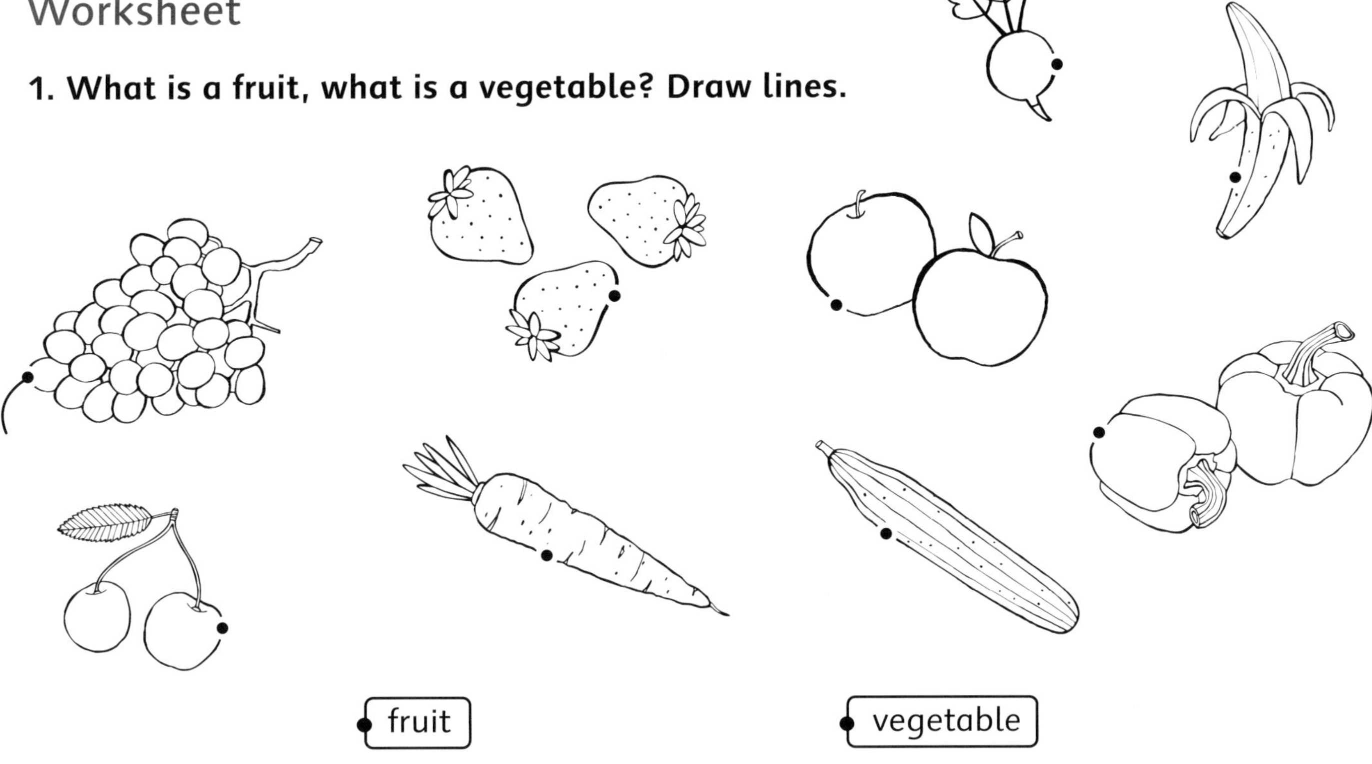

fruit

vegetable

2. Make 8 words.

First part	Second part
po- pep- cauli- mush- toma- on- gra- ra-	-per -room -to, -ion -dish -pes -flower -tato

....

....

3. Cut out and glue together. What is it?

Name

Datum

Oscar's tablet is lost (1/2)

Story

Oscar is in his room. He wants to play a game on his tablet.
But Oscar cannot find his tablet.

Start at number 1.

1 Where is the tablet?
First, Oscar looks at his **desk**.

2 The tablet is not under the carpet. Oscar looks behind the **door**.

3 This is not a chair; it is an **armchair**. Read number 11 again.

4 This is the **window**. Oscar does not look here. Read again.

5 Oscar looks under the chair – no tablet. He looks into the **wardrobe**.

6 There are only books on the bookshelf. Oscar looks behind the **sofa**.

7 The tablet is not behind the door.
Oscar no longer knows where to look. He sits down on his **bed**.

8 This is a **lamp**. You are wrong here. Read again.

Oscar's tablet is lost (2/2)

9 These are the **curtains**. Oscar does not look here. Read again.

10 The tablet is not in the wardrobe. Oscar is confused.
Maybe it is under the **carpet**?

11 Oscar cannot find the tablet behind the sofa. Where can it be?
Maybe it is under the **chair**?

12 Oscar sits on his bed. But … what is that?
There is something under the **pillow**!

13 This is the desk. But the tablet is not there.
Maybe it is on the **bookshelf**?

14 This is a **table**, not a desk. Read number 1 again.

15 The tablet is under the **pillow**! Oscar is very happy.

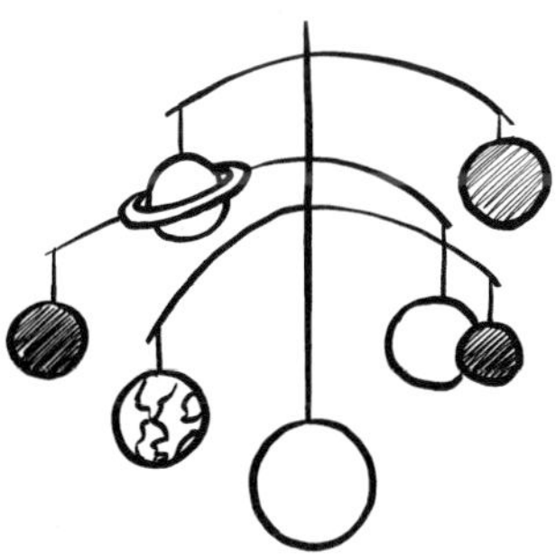

Reading steps: (1) ( ) ( ) ( ) ( ) ( ) ( ) ( ) ( ) ( )

Solution word: Oscar has got a ………… ………… ………… ………… ………… …………
………… ………… ………… ………… .

Name

Datum

Oscar's tablet is lost (1/2)

Story

Oscar is in his room and his homework is done. He wants to play a new game on his tablet, but Oscar can't find his tablet. He looks around …

Start at number 1.

1. Where is the tablet? First, Oscar looks at his desk. Usually, the tablet is there.

2. Yes, this is the carpet. But of course, the tablet isn't under it – too bad! Now Oscar looks behind the door.

3. This isn't a desk chair, it's an armchair. Oscar likes to watch TV there. Read number eleven again.

4. This is the window, but Oscar doesn't look for his tablet here. Read again carefully.

5. Oscar looks under the chair, but there is no tablet. Maybe it's in his jacket? He looks into the wardrobe.

6. On the bookshelf there are only a lot of books, but not Oscar's tablet. He turns around and looks behind the sofa.

7. The tablet isn't behind the door. Now Oscar no longer knows where to look. He is very sad and sits down on his bed.

8. This is a lamp. Oscar doesn't look here. Read again carefully.

Oscar's tablet is lost (2/2)

9 These are the curtains at the window. Sorry, you are wrong here. Read again carefully.

10 Yes, Oscar looks into the wardrobe. But the tablet isn't there. Oscar is very confused now. Maybe it's under the carpet?

11 Oscar can't find the tablet behind the sofa. Where else can it be? Oscar has an idea. He looks under the desk chair.

12 Oscar sits on his bed. The tablet is lost! But … what's that? There is something hard under the big pillow!

13 The tablet isn't on the desk, there are only pencils. Maybe it's on the bookshelf next to all the books?

14 This isn't Oscar's desk, it's a table. Read number one again.

15 Yes! Finally! Oscar's tablet is under the big pillow! Oscar is very happy and starts to play a new game.

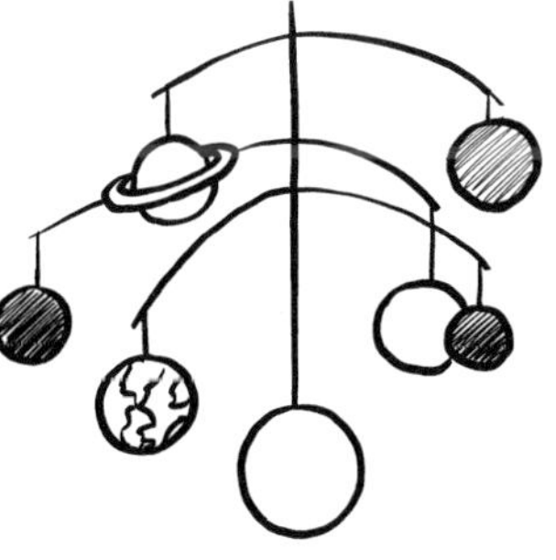

Reading steps: (1) ( ) ( ) ( ) ( ) ( ) ( ) ( ) ( ) ( )

Solution word: Oscar has got a ....

....

Oscar's tablet is lost

Answer key

1	stands for	R
2	stands for	R
3	stands for	I
4	stands for	T
5	stands for	E
6	stands for	C
7	stands for	O
8	stands for	E
9	stands for	N
10	stands for	T
11	stands for	K
12	stands for	O
13	stands for	O
14	stands for	D
15	stands for	M

Oscar's tablet is lost

List of words

English	German
again	noch einmal
answer key	Lösungsschlüssel
armchair	Ohrensessel
behind	hinter
bookshelf	Bücherregal
carefully	sorgfältig, aufmerksam
carpet	Teppich
confused	verwirrt
curtains	Vorhänge
desk	Schreibtisch
done	fertig
finally	endlich
first	als Erstes
game	Spiel
hard	hart
idea	Idee
jacket	Jacke
(to) look around	sich umsehen
lost	verschwunden
next to	neben
no longer	nicht länger, nicht mehr
of course	natürlich
pillow	Kissen
rocket	Rakete
(to) sit down	sitzen
Too bad!	Schade!
(to) turn around	umdrehen
usually	normalerweise
wardrobe	Kleiderschrank
(to) watch TV	Fernsehen gucken
Where (else) can it be?	Wo kann es (noch) sein?

Oscar's tablet is lost

Reading comprehension

⊗ Tick the right box.

1. Oscar is in
- ☐ his room.
- ☐ the bathroom.
- ☐ the living room.

2. He wants to play
- ☐ with his friend.
- ☐ the guitar.
- ☐ a game on his tablet.

3. First, he looks
- ☐ behind the sofa.
- ☐ at his desk.
- ☐ under the pillow.

4. In Oscar's bookshelf are
- ☐ only books.
- ☐ only comics.
- ☐ only magazines.

5. Oscar looks
- ☐ behind the wardrobe.
- ☐ into the wardrobe.
- ☐ under the wardrobe.

6. Oscar sits down on
- ☐ his chair.
- ☐ his bed.
- ☐ his sofa.

7. The tablet is
- ☐ under the bed.
- ☐ under the pillow.
- ☐ under the carpet.

8. Finally Oscar is
- ☐ very sad.
- ☐ very happy.
- ☐ very angry.

Oscar's tablet is lost

Worksheet

1. Draw lines.

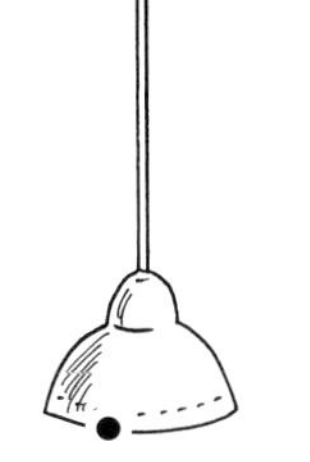

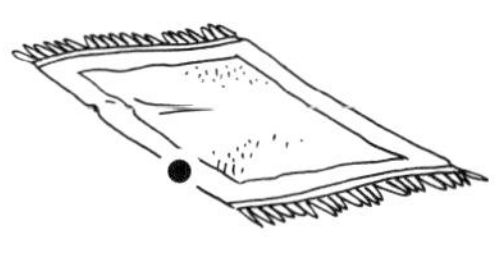

• desk • carpet • wardrobe • shelf • pillow • chair • lamp

2. Find 7 furniture words. Circle.

G	B	B	D	S	S	D	N
T	E	D	S	C	O	E	M
A	D	H	K	H	F	S	S
B	D	Q	P	A	A	K	A
L	J	M	S	I	I	H	G
E	I	C	Λ	R	P	E	T
W	A	R	D	R	O	B	E

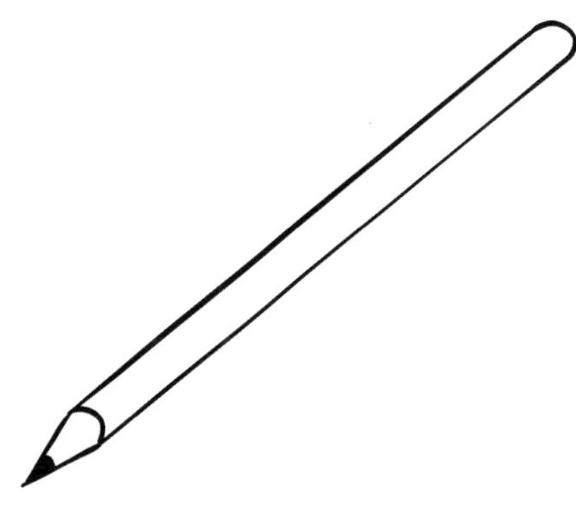

3. Write and draw.

In my room I have got … ....

....

....

....

....

....

Name

Datum

My family (1/2)

Story

Hi, my name is Lina. Today it is my 10th birthday.
All my family members are there.

Start at number 1.

1 I love my birthday! **Next to me** is my **mother**.
Her name is Marie.

2 This is my father Peter. We also have a **grandmother**, Lisbeth.
She always wears **dresses**.

3 This is not grandfather David. It is our **neighbour** Sam.
Read number 10 again.

4 This is baby Henry. And I invited our **great grandmother** Margret.
She is very, very **old**.

5 This is not my brother, it is my **cousin** Toni. Read number 7 again.

6 Very good, this is our dog, Archie. My older **sister** Ava is here, too.
She has got **short hair**.

7 Yes, this is my mother. My **brother's** name is Paul.
He has got a **cap**.

8 This is my old great grandmother Margret. We have got a **dog**, too.

My family (2/2)

9 This is not our dog. It is our neighbour's **cat**. Read number 8 again.

10 Nice, this is grandmother Lisbeth. And there is **grandfather** David. He wears glasses.

11 This is not my sister. This is my **cousin**. My sister has got short hair. Read number 6 again.

12 Yes, this is my little brother Paul. Next to my mother is my **father**. His name is Peter.

13 This is not my mother. This is my **aunt**. My mother is next to me. Read number 1 again.

14 Yes, this is my **sister** Ava. I love my family!

15 Yes, this is grandfather David.
Oh, and of course we have **baby** Henry.

Reading steps: (1) ( ) ( ) ( ) ( ) ( ) ( ) ( ) ( ) ( )

Solution word: Our last name is

....

Name

Datum

My family (1/2)

Story

Hi, nice to meet you! My name is Lina and today is my 10th birthday. There is a party in our garden and all my family members are there.

Start at number 1.

1 I love my birthday! Next to me, you can see my mother. Her name is Marie. She loves birthday parties.

2 This is my father. He loves cooking. We also have a grandmother. Her name is Lisbeth. She always wears nice dresses.

3 This isn't grandfather David. This is our neighbour Sam. He doesn't have glasses. Read number ten again.

4 This is our baby Henry. He is 6 months old. And I invited our great grandmother Margret. She is very, very old: 91 years!

5 This isn't my brother. This boy doesn't have a cap. This is my cousin Toni. Read number seven again.

6 Very good, this is our dog Archie. He is really cute. My older sister Ava is here, too. She loves pets and has got short hair.

7 Yes, this is my mother. I have a younger brother, too. His name is Paul and he has got a cool cap.

8 This is my old great grandmother Margret. We have got a dog, too. His name is Archie and he is five years old.

My family (2/2)

9 This isn't our dog, it's our neighbour's cat. Read number eight again.

10 Yes, this is grandmother Lisbeth. Her husband is our grandfather David. He wears glasses.

11 This isn't my sister. My sister has got short hair. This is my sporty cousin Grace. Read number six again.

12 Yes, this is my younger brother Paul. He is 7 years old and loves cycling. Next to my mother is my father. His name is Peter.

13 This isn't my mother. My mother is next to me. This is our aunt Kate with her wife and children. Read number one again.

14 Good, this is my older sister Ava. We are a happy family!

15 Yes, this is grandfather David. He loves reading the newspaper. Oh, and of course we have our baby Henry.

Reading steps: (1) ( ) ( ) ( ) ( ) ( ) ( ) ( ) ( ) ( )

Solution word: Our last name is

....

My family

Answer key

1	stands for	R
2	stands for	H
3	stands for	P
4	stands for	D
5	stands for	L
6	stands for	O
7	stands for	I
8	stands for	S
9	stands for	M
10	stands for	A
11	stands for	W
12	stands for	C
13	stands for	Y
14	stands for	N
15	stands for	R

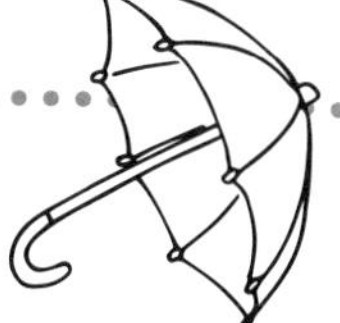

My family

List of words

English	German
again	noch einmal
always	immer
answer key	Lösungsschlüssel
aunt	Tante
cooking	Kochen
cute	niedlich
cycling	Fahrradfahren
dresses	Kleider
family members	Familienmitglieder
glasses	Brille
great grandmother	Urgroßmutter, Uroma
husband	Ehemann
(to) invite	einladen
months	Monate
neighbour	Nachbar
newspaper	Tageszeitung
next to	neben
of course	natürlich
older	ältere
pets	Haustiere
short	kurz
sporty	sportlich
(to) wear	tragen
wife	Ehefrau
younger	jünger

My family

Reading comprehension

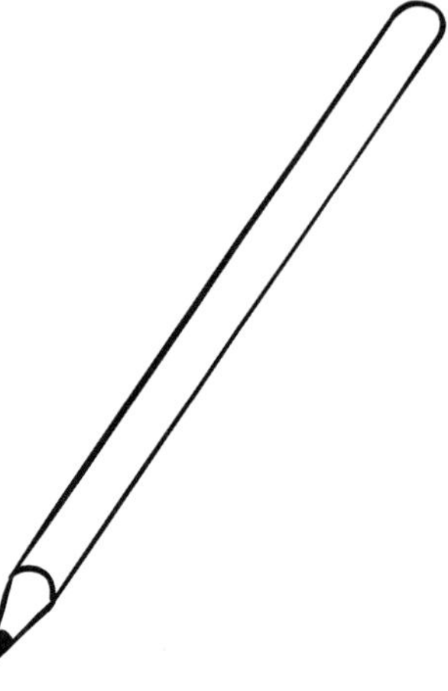

ⓧ **Tick the right box.**

1. It is Lina's
- ☐ 10th birthday.
- ☐ 8th birthday.
- ☐ 11th birthday.

2. Lina's brother Paul has got
- ☐ a scarf.
- ☐ glasses.
- ☐ a cap.

3. Lina's grandmother always wears
- ☐ jeans.
- ☐ dresses.
- ☐ skirts.

4. Lina's family has got a pet. It is
- ☐ a cat.
- ☐ a dog.
- ☐ a budgie.

5. Lina's family has got a pet. It is called
- ☐ Alex.
- ☐ Adam.
- ☐ Archie.

6. Lina's older sister Ava has got
- ☐ short hair.
- ☐ long hair.
- ☐ curly hair.

7. The names of Lina's grandparents are
- ☐ Margret and David.
- ☐ Lisbeth and Peter.
- ☐ Lisbeth and David.

8. Lina's youngest brother is
- ☐ Paul.
- ☐ Henry.
- ☐ Archie.

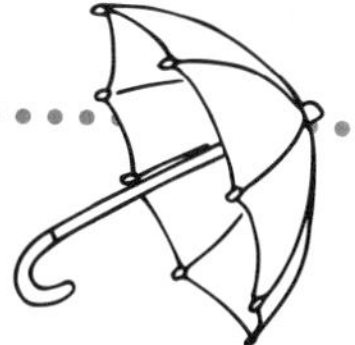

My family

Worksheet

1. Fill in the right words.

1. This is me.
2. This is my ....
3. This is my ....
4. This is my ....
5. This is my ....
6. This is my ....
7. This is my ....

brother | mother | grandmother | father | sister | grandfather

2. Find the family words. Circle.

fatherdaughtersistermotherauntbrothercousingrandfatherson

3. Read and draw lines.

My uncle •	• is the son of my parents.
My brother •	• is older than my mother.
My grandmother •	• is the daughter of my father and mother.
My sister •	• is the brother of my father or mother.

4. Me and my family. Write.

My name is ....

I am .... years old.

My mother's name ....

My father's name is ....

I have .... sister(s) and .... brother(s).

Lesespurkarte

Name der Lesespur:

....

Nummer Schlüsselwort/Schlüsselwörter

1

Lesespurkarte

Name der Lesespur:

....

Nummer Schlüsselwort/Schlüsselwörter

1

Einfache Lesespurgeschichten für den **Englischunterricht** 56

© Verlag an der Ruhr | Autorinnen: Ricarda Dransmann, Svenja Sölter
www.verlagruhr.de | Illustrationen: Bettina Weyland

Lösungen der Lesespuren

In the pet shop

1 Maja's mother,
15 cat,
4 shop assistant,
10 dog,
7 fishes,
3 fish tank,
8 guinea pig,
13 budgie,
11 bird cage,
14 money

Solution words: **grains** and **corn**

A crazy school day

1 Mrs. Miller,
10 girl with comic,
4 coloured pencils,
8 black pencil case,
9 boy with ruler,
7 glue stick,
13 scissors,
15 girl under table,
12 bin on table,
14 blackboard

Solution word: **paint brush**

Lösungen der Lesespuren

In the shopping mall

(1) (8) (2) (6) (11) (13) (5) (14) (12) (15)

1 Linda and her father,
8 dress,
2 tights,
6 T-shirt,
11 skirt,
13 cap,
5 shoes,
14 white socks,
12 jeans,
15 shop assistant

Solution word: **sweatshirt**

At the market

(1) (5) (8) (3) (6) (10) (4) (11) (9) (15)

1 Mr. Baker,
5 apples,
8 bananas,
3 grapes,
6 potatoes,
10 carrots,
4 onion,
11 peas,
9 tomatoes,
15 basket

Solution word: **pineapples**

Lösungen der Lesespuren

Oscar's tablet is lost

1 Oscar,
13 desk,
6 bookshelf,
11 sofa,
5 chair,
10 wardrobe,
2 carpet,
7 door,
12 bed,
15 pillow

Solution word: **rocket room**

My family

1 Lina,
7 mother (next to Lina),
12 brother (with cap),
2 father (next to mother),
10 grandmother (with dress),
15 grandfather (with glasses),
4 baby,
8 old great grandmother,
6 dog,
14 sister (with short hair)

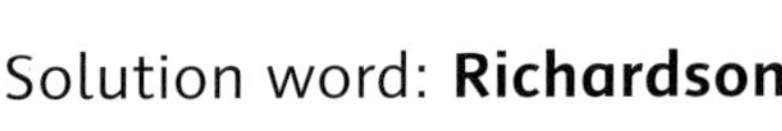

Solution word: **Richardson**

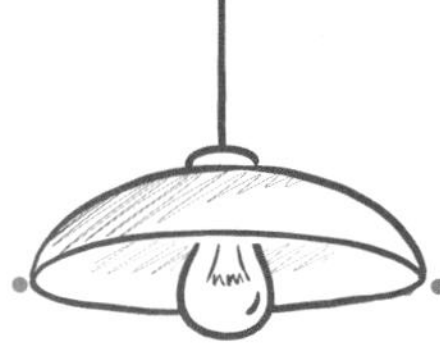

Lösungen – Reading comprehension

In the pet shop, S. 14

⊗ Tick the right box.

1. Maja wants **a new pet**.

2. Maja's mother likes **the cat**.

3. The dog is **too big**.

4. The fish tank is **too expensive**.

5. Maja can't buy the guinea pig because **it is already sold**.

6. Maja's new pet needs **a bird cage**.

7. Maja pays with her **birthday money**.

8. Maja's new pet is **a budgie**.

A crazy school day, S. 22

⊗ Tick the right box.

1. The teacher is called **Mrs. Miller**.

2. Susan reads **a comic**.

3. The coloured pencils are **on the floor**.

4. Susan´s pencil case is **black**.

5. A boy takes a ruler to stick something on **a piece of paper**.

6. Jim cuts his bread **with his scissors**.

7. The bin is **on the table**.

8. The blackboard says **it is Sunday**.

Lösungen – Reading comprehension

In the shopping mall, S. 30

⊗ Tick the right box.

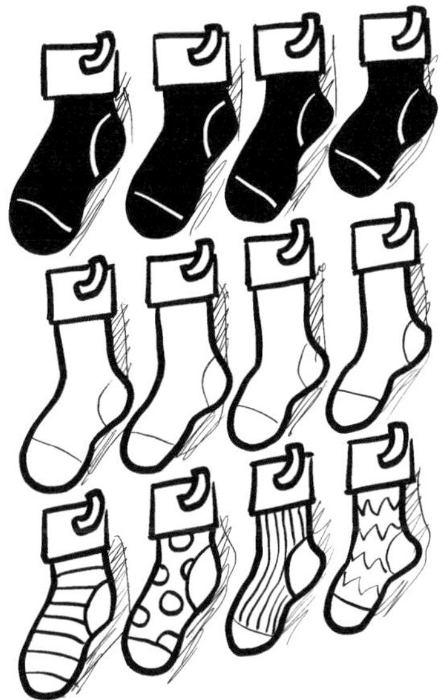

1. Linda is in the shopping mall with **her father**.

2. Linda tries on a dress with **flowers**.

3. Linda takes a T-shirt **with dots**.

4. The skirt is **too small**.

5. Linda's father sees new **white socks**.

6. Linda's father does not want **new jeans.**

7. At the end, Linda's father is **tired**.

8. Linda and her father pay at the shop assistant and **go home**.

At the market, S. 38

⊗ Tick the right box.

1. The Bakers go to **the market**.

2. The family wants to make **a potato soup**.

3. The Bakers buy fruits for **a smoothie**.

4. The Bakers are **Mr. Baker, Jenny and Ron**.

5. Mr. Baker wants to buy **8 potatoes**.

6. The carrots look **fantastic**.

7. Jenny does not like **tomatoes**.

8. The fruits and vegetables are in **the basket**.

Lösungen – Reading comprehension

Oscar's tablet is lost, S. 46

⊗ **Tick the right box.**

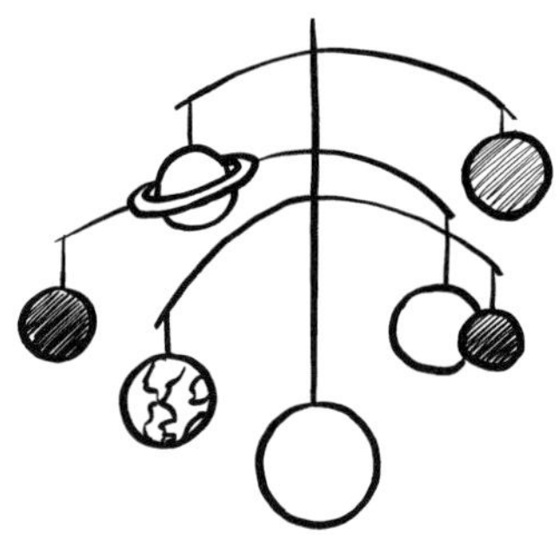

1. Oscar is in **his room**.

2. He wants to play **a game on his tablet**.

3. First, he looks **at his desk**.

4. In Oscar's bookshelf are **only books**.

5. Oscar looks **into the wardrobe**.

6. Oscar sits down on **his bed**.

7. The tablet is **under the pillow**.

8. Finally Oscar is **very happy**.

My family, S. 54

⊗ **Tick the right box.**

1. It is Lina's **10th birthday.**

2. Lina's brother Paul has got **a cap.**

3. Lina's grandmother always wears **dresses.**

4. Lina's family has got a pet. It is **a dog.**

5. Lina's family has got a pet. It is called **Archie.**

6. Lina's older sister Ava has got **short hair.**

7. The names of Lina's grandparents are **Lisbeth and David.**

8. Lina's youngest brother is **Henry**.

Lösungen – worksheet

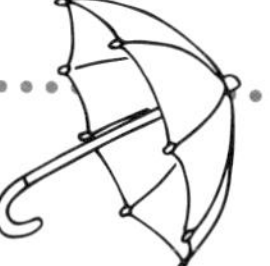

In the pet shop

Worksheet

1. Write the correct numbers.

(1) parrot	(2) cat	(3) dog
(4) fish	(5) mouse	(6) rabbit
(7) guinea pig	(8) budgie	(9) tortoise

2. Find the pet words. Circle.

mouse|fish|guineapig|cat|budgie|rabbit|dog|tortoise|parrot|hamster

3. Read and draw.

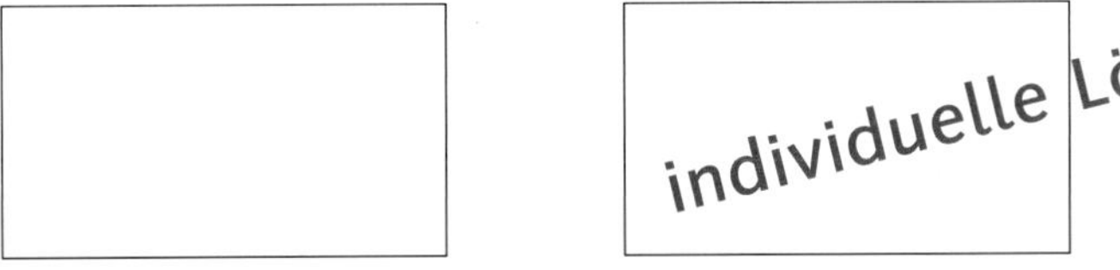

two brown cats

four yellow fishes

a colourful parrot

4. What's your favourite pet? Write and draw.

My favourite pet is ....

individuelle Lösung

© Verlag an der Ruhr | Autorinnen: Ricarda Dransmann, Svenja Sölter
www.verlagruhr.de | Illustrationen: Bettina Weyland

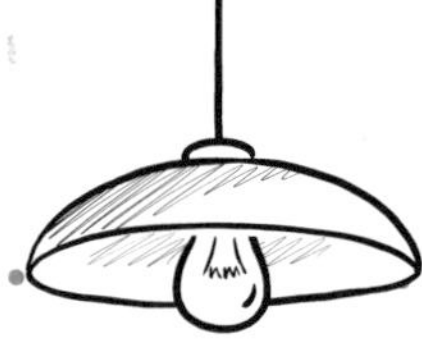

Lösungen – worksheet

A crazy school day

Worksheet

1. Fill in the right words.

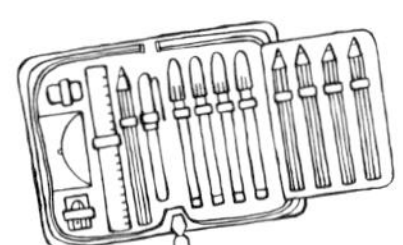

pencil case

glue

blackboard

scissors

pencil

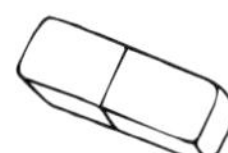

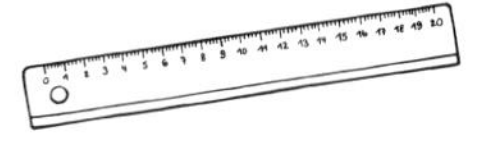

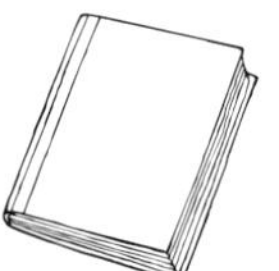

rubber

ruler

book

ruler | book | pencil case | 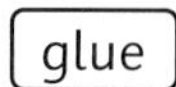 glue | scissors | blackboard | rubber | pencil

2. Find the school words. Circle.

rubber|schoolbag|glue|ruler|book|pencil|blackboard|scissors

3. Do you know the school words? Write.

okbo **book**

luerr **ruler**

clinpe **pencil**

ssssicro **scissors**

ckalbbardo **blackboard**

buberr **rubber**

4. Write about your school bag.

In my school bag there are ....

individuelle Lösung

Einfache Lesespurgeschichten für den **Englischunterricht**  23

© Verlag an der Ruhr | Autorinnen: Ricarda Dransmann, Svenja Sölter
www.verlagruhr.de | Illustrationen: Anja Boretzki (alles außer Regenschirm)

Lösungen – worksheet

In the shopping mall

Worksheet

1. Draw lines.

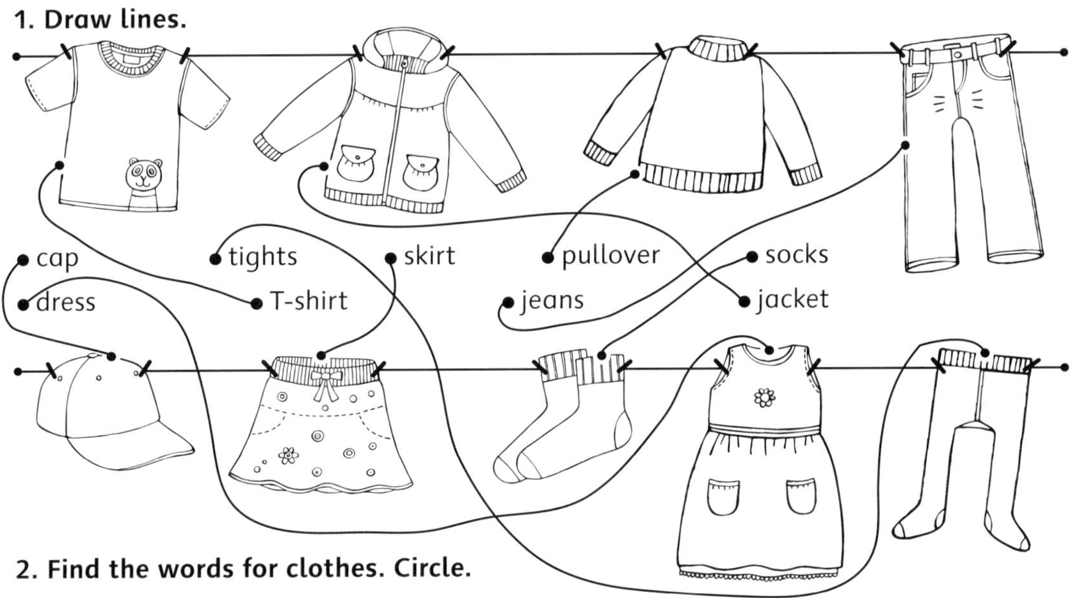

2. Find the words for clothes. Circle.

dress|tights|socks|skirt|scarf|jeans|cap|shoes|pullover|jacket

3. Find the odd one out. Circle.

a) jacket – pullover – (socks) – T-shirt
b) (T-shirt) – trousers – jeans – tights
c) trousers – (skirt) – shorts – jeans
d) socks – shorts – trousers – (cap)

4. Fill in the right words.

pullover (2x)
shoes
stripes
shopping mall
shop assistant

Jonas and his mother are in the **shopping mall**.

Jonas says, "For winter, I need a warm **pullover**."

Jonas takes a **pullover** with **stripes**.

His mother says, "And look at your old sneakers!

You need new **shoes**, too." At the end, Jonas

and his mother pay at the **shop assistant** and go home.

Lösungen – worksheet

At the market

Worksheet

1. What is a fruit, what is a vegetable? Draw lines.

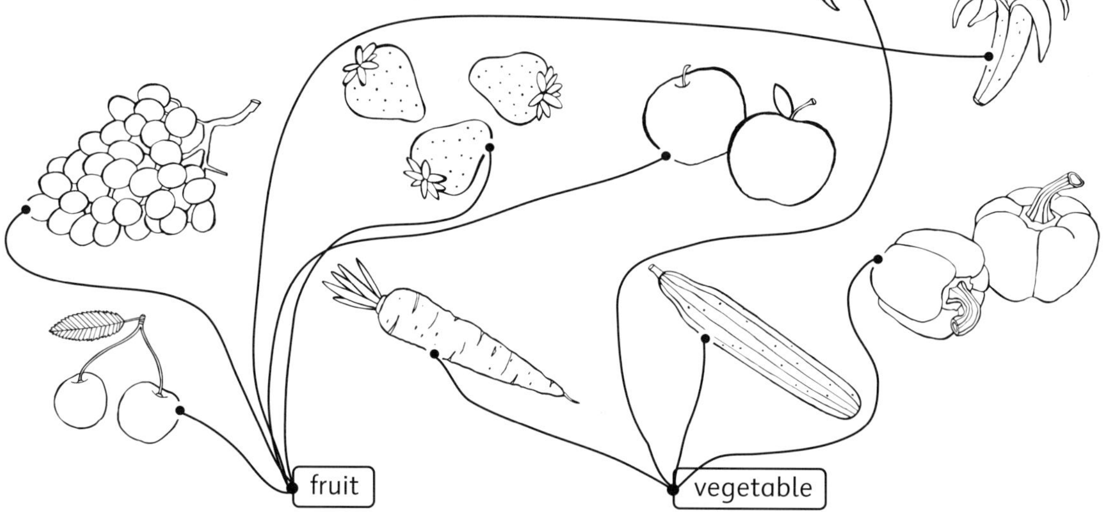

2. Make 8 words.

First part	Second part
po- pep- cauli- mush- toma- on- gra- ra-	-per -room -to, -ion -dish -pes -flower -tato

potato, pepper, mushroom, grapes, tomato, cauliflower, radish, onion

3. Cut out and glue together. What is it?

It is a cauliflower.

Lösungen – worksheet

Oscar's tablet is lost

Worksheet

1. Draw lines.

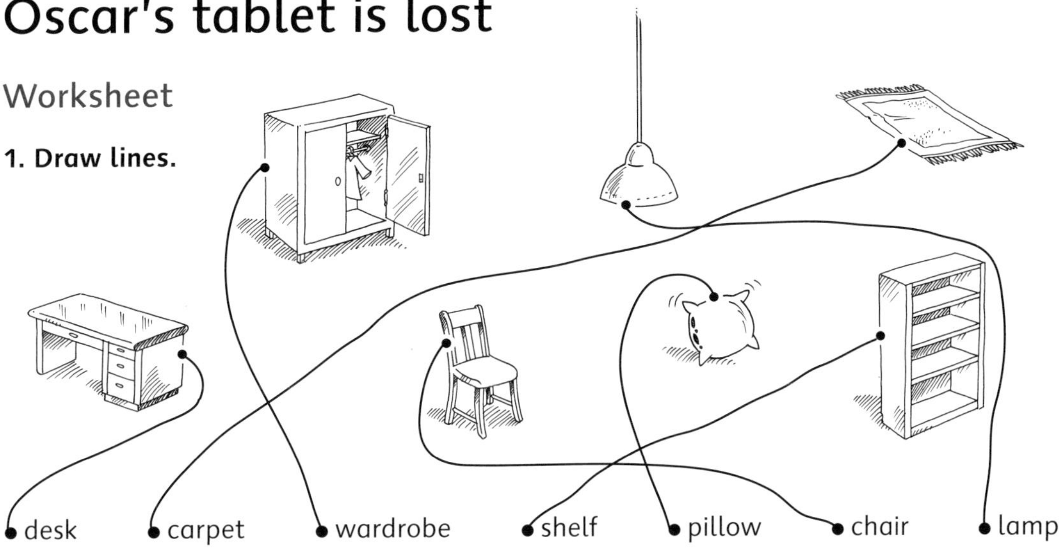

desk carpet wardrobe shelf pillow chair lamp

2. Find 7 furniture words. Circle.

G	B	B	D	S	S	D	N
T	E	D	S	C	O	E	M
A	D	H	K	H	F	S	S
B	D	Q	P	A	A	K	A
L	J	M	S	I	I	H	G
E	I	C	A	R	P	E	T
W	A	R	D	R	O	B	E

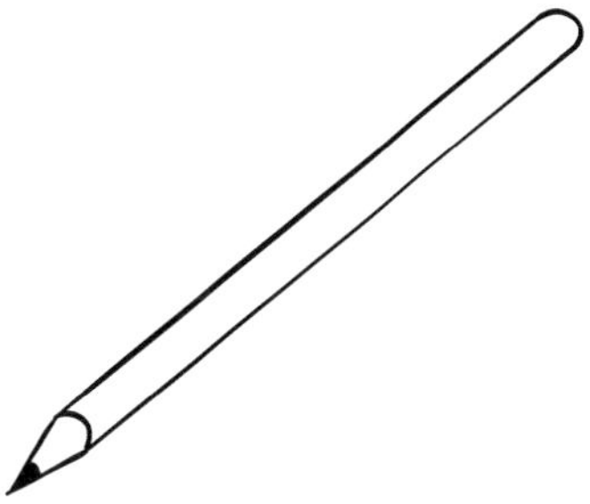

3. Write and draw.

In my room I have got …

individuelle Lösung

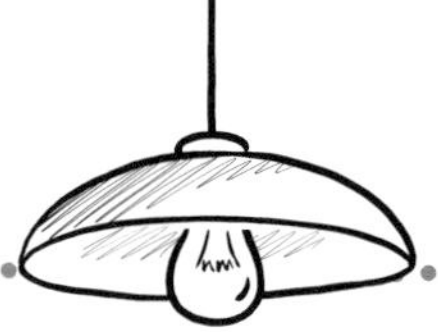

Lösungen – worksheet

My family

Worksheet

1. Fill in the right words.

1. This is me.
2. This is my **sister**.
3. This is my **grandfather**.
4. This is my **mother**.
5. This is my **father**.
6. This is my **grandmother**.
7. This is my **brother**.

brother | mother | grandmother | father | sister | grandfather

2. Find the family words. Circle.

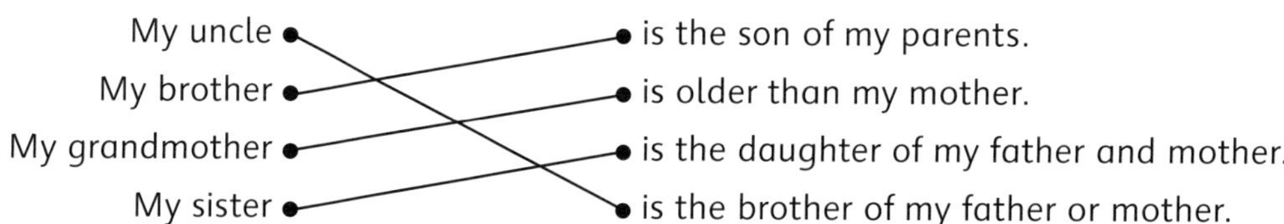

father|daughter|sister|mother|aunt|brother|cousin|grandfather|son

3. Read and draw lines.

My uncle – is the brother of my father or mother.
My brother – is the son of my parents.
My grandmother – is older than my mother.
My sister – is the daughter of my father and mother.

4. Me and my family. Write.

My name is ....

I am .... years old.

My mother's name ....

My father's name is ....

I have .... sister(s) and .... brother(s).

individuelle Lösung

Einfache Lesespurgeschichten für den **Englischunterricht** 55

13
3
11
2
7
12
6
9
Ted
1
4
10
14
5
15
8

51+49=

SUNDAY

1×1

51+49=

1 2 3 4 5 6 7 8 9 10 11 12 13 14 15

1
2
3
4
5
6
7
8
9
10
11
12
13
14
15
KEN
LIV

1 2 3 4 5 6 7 8 9 10 11 12 13 14 15

1 2 3 4 5 6 7 8 9 10 11 12 13 14 15

GARDEN HOUSE
1
2
3
4
5
6
7
8
9
10
11
12
13
14
15

51+49 =
SUNDAY
1×1
51+49=
1
2
3
4
5
6
7
8
9
10
11
12
13
14
15

1
2
3
4
5
6
7
8
9
10
11
12
13
14
15
KEN
LIV

1
10
4
6
14
9
13
7
11
12
15
8
5
2
3

1
2
3
4
5
6
7
8
9
10
11
12
13
14
15

GARDEN HOUSE
HAPPY BIRTHDAY
1
2
3
4
5
6
7
8
9
10
11
12
13
14
15